张
张马田
张妈妈
张美丽
张爸爸
陈小玲家
陈爸爸
陈妈妈
陈小玲
Arun's family
Lata
Arun
Dad
Mum
Anna's family
Anna
Dad
Mum
Peter

我的

第一课 C2/M47

李大山：这是我的学校，我的学校不大，我们有一百多个学生，二十多个老师。学校有一个很大的图书馆。我们可以在那里看书和做功课。

Sentence construction

The use of 多 after a number (usually ten's, hundred's etc) to indicate more than that number:
Number + 多 + measure word + noun
eg: 十 + 多 + 条 + 鱼 ⇨ 十多条鱼
eg: 一百 + 多 + 个 + 学生 ⇨ 一百多个学生

To ask for permission to do something, you say:
Subject + model + verb + 吗?
eg: 我 + 可以 + 去公园 + 吗?
⇨ 我可以去公园吗?
To answer, you say: 可以 or 不可以

一起来认字

C3/M48

多 many
图书馆 library
教室 classroom
礼堂 assembly hall

Remember these phrases? 学校 学生 老师 这是 那是
上 年级 运动场 电脑

学校

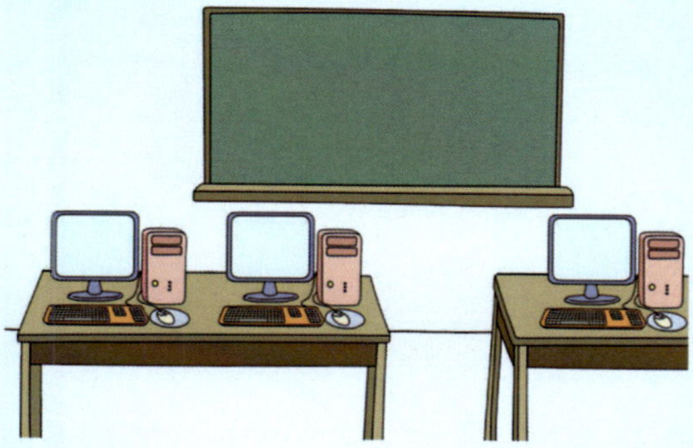

张马田：我们的学校有两个电脑室，我们可以在那里上网。

Lata：我们有一个很大的食堂，我们在那里吃午饭。

Jasmine：我们有十多个教室，我们在那里上课。

To say you can, as able to, do something in a certain place, you say:
Subject + model + 在 + place + verb
eg: 我 + 可以 + 在 + 花园 + 踢球 ⇨ 我可以在花园踢球。
eg: 学生 + 可以 + 在 + 图书馆 + 看书 ⇨ 学生可以在图书馆看书。

食堂 canteen
室 room
教 teach
百 hundred
可以 can
上课 attend lesson

Question phrases to practise
什么 你在图书馆做什么？ 学生可以在教室做什么？
谁 你和谁一起在运动场打球？

A. 用英文回答问题

Listen to the recording and answer in English.

1. Whose computer is this? ……………………
2. Whose school bag is this? ……………………
3. Whose pencil is that? ……………………
4. Whose teacher is that? ……………………

B. 在图画里找答案

Listen to the questions and find the answers in the picture.

介绍你的学校

Look at the table below and talk about the school of each child's. After that you can tell the class about your own.

我的学校有一百多个学生，二十多个老师。学校有一个很大的图书馆、一个电脑室、十二个教室，还有一个食堂。

Number of	大山	Amir	Chrissy	月冬
pupils	100+	700+	500+	120+
teachers	20+	60+	40+	25+
library	1	4	3	2
classrooms	12	25	30	20
computer rooms	1	8	6	3
sports grounds				
halls				
canteens	1	2	1	1

第一课

A. 填上正确答案 Label the pictures using the phrases given.

电脑室　食堂　运动场　图书馆　教室　礼堂

1 ....

2 ....

3 ....

4 ....

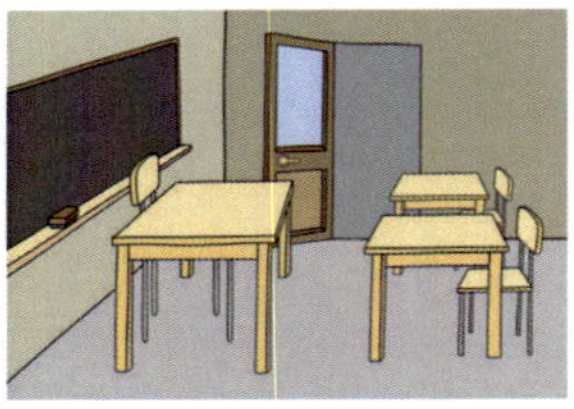

5 ....

6 ....

B. 去哪里报名？ 画线连起来 Saturday is activity day in the school. Pupils must go to different rooms to register their wish to join different activities.

1. 张马田 and Richard must go to the sports ground to join the football team.
2. Jasmine must go to the assembly hall to join the kite-making club.
3. Lata and Anna must go to the computer room to join the badminton team.
4. 张美丽 must go to the canteen to learn how to make a cake.
5. 月冬 must go to Year 4's classroom to join the painting group.
6. 陈小玲 must go to the library to enrol to swim.

画画 •	• 电脑室
游泳 •	• 四年级教室
打羽毛球 •	• 运动场
踢足球 •	• 礼堂
做蛋糕 •	• 食堂
做风筝 •	• 图书馆

基本字形 Basic shapes

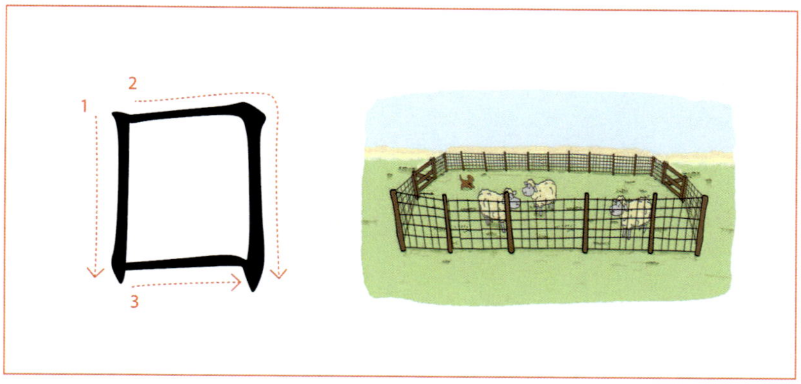

This shape 囗 looks like 口 but is bigger. Characters with this shape usually have something to do with limits and enclosures. Can you see 囗 in 园, 图, 国, 围.

Use a red pen to go over the 囗 in each character.

园 图 国 围

Now practise writing these characters.

园	园	园	园	园	园	园	园	园	园
图	图	图	图	图	图	图	图	图	图
国	国	国	国	国	国	国	国	国	国
围	围	围	围	围	围	围	围	围	围

今天

第二课 C6/M51

李大山：我喜欢晴天，我可以和我的家人一起去爬山。

Richard: 我喜欢阴天，我可以在家看书。

Sentence construction

Subject + model + verb
eg: 我可以去

一起来认字

C7/M52

晴天 clear day
下雪 snow
下雨 rain
有风 windy

Remember these phrases? 风筝 花园 公园 海滩 打羽毛球

下雨

张马田：我喜欢下雪天，姐姐和我可以在花园里堆雪人。

Jasmine：我不喜欢下雨天，我不可以去公园打羽毛球。

陈小玲：今天有风，我可以去公园放风筝。

阴天 cloudy　　爬山 to climb mountain　　雪人 snowman

下毛毛雨 drizzle　　堆 to pile up

Question phrases to practise	谁	晴天你和谁一起做什么？
	什么	下雨天你做什么？

A. 填上正确答案 Write the correct numbers in the brackets as you hear them read out.

(　　) (　　) (　　) (　　) (　　)

B. 选出正确图画，把答案写在横线上

What is the weather like? What are they doing?

1 ....

2 ....

3 ....

4 ....

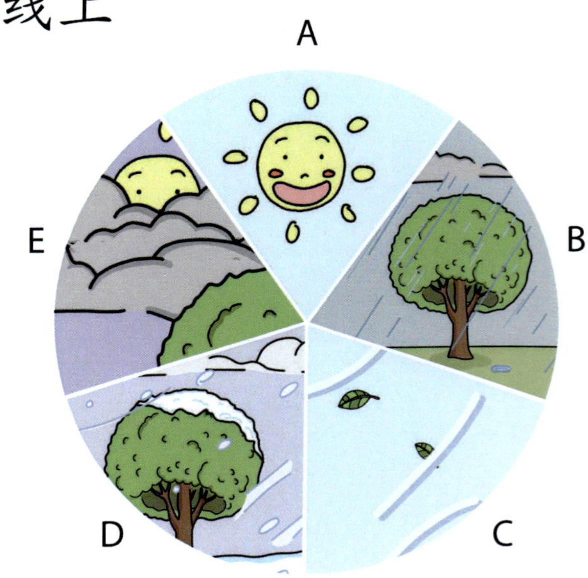

C. 回答问题 Listen to the recording and answer the questions.

1. Where did 李大山 go yesterday? ....
2. Who went with 李大山? ....
3. What was the weather like? ....
4. What did they do? ....
5. How did they like this outing? Why? ....

猜谜语 What is it?

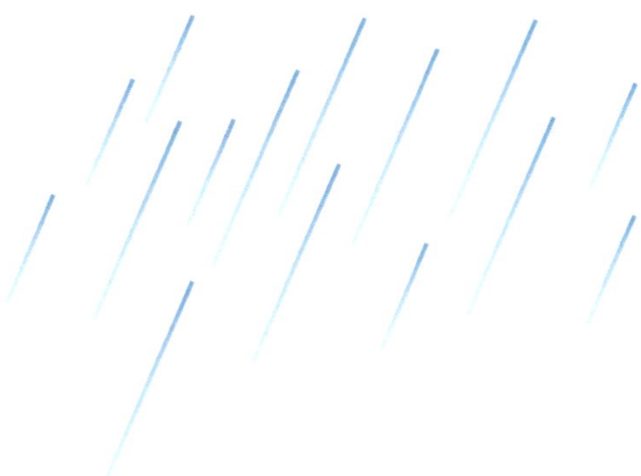

千条线，
万条线，
落到河里都不见。

谜底 ....

一朵，两朵，三朵
四朵，五朵，六朵
落到地上都不见。

谜底 ....

猜一字 What is this character?

大雨落在横山上

字 ....

朋友半边不见了

字 ....

第二课

A. 画线连起来

Draw a line to link the weather to the characters.

晴天　　下雨　　下雪　　有风　　阴天

B. 哪幅图画配哪个句子？

Match the pictures to the sentences.

A (　　　　)

B (　　　　)

C (　　　　)

D (　　　　)

1. 昨晚下了大雪，今天李大山和妹妹在花园堆雪人。
2. 下雨了，李大山在家看书。
3. 李大山喜欢晴天，他可以在海滩玩。
4. 今天有风，李大山去公园放风筝。

基本字形 Basic shapes

雨 means rain. Characters with this shape usually relates to a weather condition like snow 雪 and fog 雾. Can you see 雨 in 雪, 雾? Use a red pen to go over the 雨 in each character.

雨 雪 雾

Now practise writing these characters.

雨	雨	雨	雨	雨	雨	雨	雨	雨	雨
雪	雪	雪	雪	雪	雪	雪	雪	雪	雪
风	风	风	风	风	风	风	风	风	风
爬	爬	爬	爬	爬	爬	爬	爬	爬	爬
堆	堆	堆	堆	堆	堆	堆	堆	堆	堆

第三课 C10/M55

美丽的

陈小玲: Richard, 你喜欢哪个季节?

Richard: 我最喜欢春天, 春天天气暖, 花草树木都很好看! 你呢, 小玲?

Sentence construction

To say that you like something most, you use 最.
Subject + 最 + 喜欢 + something
eg: 我最喜欢红色
eg: 我最喜欢果汁

To say that you like to do something most, you say:
Subject + 最 + 喜欢 + activity
eg: 我最喜欢踢足球
eg: 我最喜欢吃汉堡包

一起来认字

C11/M56

季节 season
最 most
春天 Spring
秋天 Autumn
天气 weather
暖 warm

Remember these phrases? 夏天 热 冬天 冷 穿 风筝
公园 红 黄 地上

秋天

陈小玲: 我喜欢秋天，秋天天气凉，地上满是红叶和黄叶，十分美丽！

To say that you dislike something most or to do something most, you add 不 before 喜欢.
eg: 我最不喜欢蓝色
eg: 我最不喜欢游泳

凉 cool	满是 covered with/full of	美丽 beautiful
叶 leaf	十分 extremely	

Question phrases to practise	什么	春天天气暖，你喜欢做什么？ 地上有什么？
	哪	你最喜欢哪个季节？

第三课 C12/M57

A. 填上正确答案

Write the correct numbers in the brackets as you hear them read out.

a. Spring (   )   b. Summer (   )   c. Autumn (   )

d. Winter (   )   e. cold (   )   f. warm (   )

g. hot (   )   h. cool (   )   i. weather (   )

B. 填上正确答案

Choose the correct pictures to match the statements read out and write the numbers in the brackets.

a. (   )

b. (   )

c. (   )

d. (   )

Amir:
我最喜欢夏天，夏天我们
不用上学，我可以在海滩
玩，又可以在海里游泳。

Jamal:
我最喜欢冬天，冬天下
大雪，我们可以堆雪人。
圣诞节在冬天，我们不
用上学。

张美丽：
我最喜欢春天，花园里
和公园里都有很多美丽
的花。

张马田：
我最喜欢秋天，秋天天
气不冷也不热，秋天有
很多水果吃。

你喜欢哪一个季节？为什么？

A. 填上正确答案 Match the picture to the correct answer.

 ( )

 ( )

 ( )

 ( )

a. 冷	b. 春天	c. 凉	d. 冬天
e. 热	f. 秋天	g. 暖	h. 夏天

 ( )

 ( )

 ( )

 ( )

B. 填上正确答案 Find the correct answer to fill in the blanks.

1. 春天的花园很美丽，那里有很多______和______ ______。

2. ______ ______来了，我们可以在______ ______游泳。

3. 秋天有很多______ ______，我最喜欢吃______ ______。

4. 冬天______ ______冷，我最喜欢在下雪天______ ______ ______。

夏天	天气	海里	堆雪人
梨子	花	水果	蝴蝶

拆拆看 What's in these characters?

Chinese characters are often made up of more than one word or radical.

For example: 草 is made up of 艹 日 十
茶 is made up of 艹 人 木
哥 is made up of 可 可

Can you work out how the following characters are made up?

最 is made up of ....

暖 is made up of ....

秋 is made up of ....

蝶 is made up of ....

春 is made up of ....

季 is made up of ....

叶 is made up of ....

Now practise writing these characters.

最	最	最	最	最	最	最	最	最	最
春	春	春	春	春	春	春	春	春	春
暖	暖	暖	暖	暖	暖	暖	暖	暖	暖
季	季	季	季	季	季	季	季	季	季
秋	秋	秋	秋	秋	秋	秋	秋	秋	秋
气	气	气	气	气	气	气	气	气	气

第四课 C13/M58

我哥哥

Sentence construction

To describe someone's build, you say:
Subject + 个子 + adjective
eg: 姐姐 + 个子 + 高 ⇨ 姐姐个子高
eg: 爸爸 + 个子 + 矮 ⇨ 爸爸个子矮

To describe someone who is tall as well as slim, you say:
Subject + 又 + adjective 又 + adjective
eg: 哥哥 + 又 + 高 + 又 + 瘦 ⇨ 哥哥又高又瘦
eg: 小弟弟又胖又矮

一起来认字

C14/M59

高 tall
矮 short
胖 fat
瘦 slim

Remember these phrases? 头 眼睛 鼻子 长 短 金 黑 戴 穿 女

又高又瘦

你好！我今年也八岁，上三年级。我有黑头发和黑眼睛。我喜欢运动，每星期日我都和我姐姐一起去运动场打羽毛球。

黄大年 三月十四日

胖 瘦

高 矮

戴眼镜 棕色头发 金头发

个子 build
男 male
棕色 brown
漂亮 pretty
头发 hair
眼镜 eye-glasses

Question phrases to practise			
	什么	你在图书馆做什么？	你可以在教室做什么？
	谁	你和谁一起在运动场打球？	

第四课 C15/M60 一起来唱歌'金头发 蓝眼睛' P78

A. 填上正确答案

Listen to the recording and write the correct number in the brackets in the order you hear it.

(   )

(   )

(   )

(   )

(   )

(   )

(   )

(   )

B. 选出正确答案填在图画下面 Listen to the recording and choose the correct answers from the pictures given below.

a 

b 

c 

d 

e 

f 

g 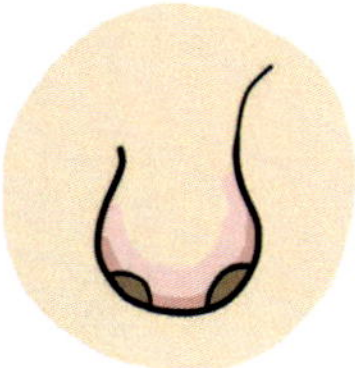

h 

i 

j 

k 

l 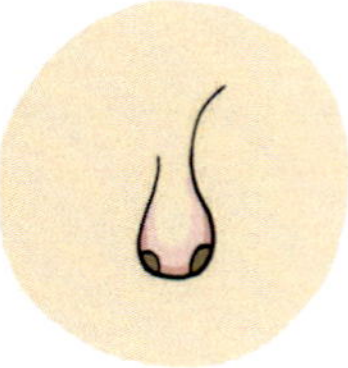

1. a,b,c ....
2. e,g,f ....
3. h,d,i ....
4. j,k ....

他们长得怎样?

Here are two new teachers 黄老师 and 白老师, and two new pupils Jack and Mary in your school. Work with a partner and take turns to describe them to each other

黄老师

白老师

Jack

Mary

A. 画线连起来 Draw lines to match the Chinese with the pictures.

耳朵	头发
眼镜	眼睛
鼻子	口

B. 找相反词 Match the opposites.

高	胖	小	黑	短	冷	新
白	矮	瘦	旧	热	大	长

C. 你可以帮忙吗？ The police are looking for two suspects. Can you help them draw a photo-fit for each according to the description below?

WANTED

矮胖女人，金色短发，大眼睛，穿红色毛衣、蓝色裙子、黑鞋。

高个子男人，大鼻子，没有头发，戴眼镜，穿绿色汗衫、黑色牛仔裤、白色运动鞋。

基本字形 Basic shapes

矢

矢 means arrow. Can you see 矢 in 短, 矮, 知? Use a red pen to go over the 矢 in each character.

短 矮 知

金 

金 means gold or metal. When it is used as part of a character, it looks like this: 钅 Can you see 钅 in 镜, 铅, 针? Use a blue pen to go over the 钅 in each character.

镜 铅 针

Now practise writing these characters.

短	短	短	短	短	金	金	金	金	金
矮	矮	矮	矮	矮	镜	镜	镜	镜	镜
					铅	铅	铅	铅	铅

第五课 C17/M62

我妹妹

这是我祖父,他今年六十八岁。
我祖父很胖,他喜欢讲故事
给我们听。

那是我祖母,她今年六十七岁。
我祖母很高,她比我祖父高。
她很慈祥,常常做蛋糕给我们吃。

我爸爸叫李学年,他是一个
火车司机,他很爱我和妹妹,
常常带我们去公园玩。

Sentence construction

To say someone tells us story, you use 讲 and 给:
Subject + 讲 + 故事 + 给 + object + 听
eg: 妈妈 + 讲 + 故事 + 给 + 我们 + 听
⇨ 妈妈讲故事给我们听

To say someone makes something for us to eat, you use 做 and 吃: Subject + 做 + something + 给 + someone + 吃
eg: 姐姐 + 做 + 蛋糕 + 给 + 我们 + 吃
⇨ 姐姐做蛋糕给我们吃

一起来认字

C18/M63

祖父 grandfather
祖母 grandmother
讲 tell, say
比 compare

Remember these phrases? 可爱 故事 听 蛋糕 火车 司机 护士 带 弹琴 画画 看 教

很可爱

我妈妈叫王乐风，她是一个护士。她又高又瘦，喜欢打网球。她常常跟爸爸一起去运动场打球。

这个女孩子是我妹妹，她叫李月冬。她很可爱，喜欢笑。她很爱动物，她想有一只猫。

To compare two things, you use 比:
A 比 B + adjective
eg: 祖父比祖母高
eg: 哥哥的风筝比我的风筝大

If you want to say someone does something frequently, you use 常常: Subject + 常常 + activity
eg: 张马田 + 常常 + 去公园打球
⇨ 张马田常常去公园打球

慈祥 kind
常常 often
爱 love
跟 with/and
孩子 child

Question phrases to practise
谁 谁比谁高？ 哥哥做蛋糕给谁吃？
什么 弟弟常常去海滩做什么？

A. 找相反词

Listen to the recording and find the opposite of each phrase read out.

(a) girl

(b) fat

(c) listen

(d) grandma

(e) child

(f) tall

(g) short

B. 用英文回答问题

Listen to the recording and answer the questions in English.

a. Who is a train driver? ……

b. What is Richard's dad's job? ……

c. Can Richard's dad cook Western food? ……

d. Whose dad is taller? ……

e. Who can sing? ……

f. Who can draw better? ……

介绍 Introductions

Richard talks about his grandma.

这是我的祖母，她常常做蛋糕给我们吃，她做的蛋糕很好吃。她也会唱歌和讲故事，她唱的歌和讲的故事都很好听。

Can you describe Arun's grandma and Anna's dad, using the pictures below?

介绍你的一个家人 Now you describe a family member to the class.

A. 画线连起来

Draw lines to match the Chinese with the English below.

祖母	compare
慈祥	grandpa
故事	often
祖父	child
孩子	kind
讲	story
比	grandma
常常	tell

B. 找出正确答案，把数字填在(　)内

Match the answers on the right to the questions on the left.

1. 你喜欢运动吗？
2. 昨天你跟你爸爸去了哪里？
3. 这是谁的眼镜？
4. 你喜欢你的姐姐吗？
5. 李大山的妈妈在公园做什么？
6. 谁教学生们做风筝？

(　　) 喜欢。我祖母常常带我去运动场打网球。

(　　) 她在公园散步。

(　　) 张老师。

(　　) 喜欢。她常常跟我一起玩，也会讲故事给我听。

(　　) 我们去了超级市场买东西。

(　　) 这是陈小玲爸爸的。

基本字形 Basic shapes

Remember these characters? 穿 家 它 宠 市 高 商 堂 常

Can you tell if they have anything in common? They have different 'hats' at the top.

For example:

- bobble hat 亠 as in 高
- hat with ties 亠丷 as in 商
- hat with feathers 龸 as in 常
- hat with scarf 穴 as in 穿
- hat with sides 宀 as in 家

Now practise writing these characters.

高	高	高	高	高	高	高	高	高	高
市	市	市	市	市	市	市	市	市	市
常	常	常	常	常	常	常	常	常	常
堂	堂	堂	堂	堂	堂	堂	堂	堂	堂
穿	穿	穿	穿	穿	穿	穿	穿	穿	穿
它	它	它	它	它	它	它	它	它	它
宠	宠	宠	宠	宠	宠	宠	宠	宠	宠

足球

李大山:
Richard, 明天有足球比赛, 我们的足球队对圣马田学校的足球队, 你知道吗?

Richard:
知道, 陈老师昨天跟我们说了。大山, 你是足球队的队员吗?

Sentence construction

比赛 can mean a match or a competition.
eg 羽毛球比赛、游泳比赛、唱歌比赛、画画比赛
When 比赛 is a match, you have one side against another, then you use 对,
A 队对 B 队, eg Liverpool 足球队对 Leeds 足球队.

一起来认字

C22/M67

比赛 match/competition
队员 team member
队 team
对 against

Remember these phrases? 足球 网球 羽毛球 乒乓球 游泳
画画 唱歌 放风筝 划龙舟 讲故事

比赛

李大山：是啊！我是队员。美丽，你会来看我们的足球比赛吗？

张美丽：对不起，我报名参加了跳舞比赛，明天要练习呢！

To compare more than two things, you use 比 and 最.
A 比 B 高, C 最高。
eg: 哥哥比弟弟高，爸爸最高。
eg: 我的铅笔比弟弟的铅笔长，爸爸的铅笔最长。

The use of 不 to form a question:
eg: 是不是，会不会，去不去

知道 know	报名 register	跳舞 dance
对不起 sorry	参加 take part	练习 practise

Question phrases to practise		
是不是	他是不是李老师？	
会不会	你会不会来看我们比赛？	
去不去	今天下午你去不去打球？	
几	几月几日有足球比赛？	
什么	明天有什么比赛？	
哪	明天的比赛是哪个队对哪个队？	

第六课 C23/M68

A. 什么比赛?

What competition is it?

a. (   )

b. (   )

c. (   )

d. (   )

e. (   )

f. (   )

B. 用英文回答问题

Listen to the recording and answer the questions in English.

1. Which sport has 陈小玲 taken up at school? ……………………
2. What time is the tennis match? ……………………
3. When is the football match? ……………………
4. Who will be going to see the football match? ……………………
5. Who has entered the painting competition? ……………………
6. What will they paint? ……………………
7. Which festival is coming up soon? ……………………
8. What are 马田's family going to do? ……………………

他们做什么活动?

Which activities do they do?

He practises everyday at 5pm.

李大山喜欢弹琴，他每天下午五点都练习弹琴。

Competition: 2pm on 6 May.

张马田喜欢打网球，他参加了五月六日的网球比赛。

1. Jasmine is a member of the school football team. She practises every Tuesday at 4pm.

2. 李大山's dad practises every Sunday at 9am.

3. Arun practises every Saturday at 7pm.

4. Jamal likes swimming. He is taking part in a swimming competition in school tomorrow.

A. 找出正确答案

Match the English with the Chinese phrases given below:

team member .... register .... take part ....

dance .... match ....

1. 比赛　2. 跳舞　3. 报名　4. 参加　5. 队员

B. 配词 Match the characters on the left with those on the right to make phrases.

练	期
知	舞
日	队
跳	道
球	习

C. 问和答，找找看 Match the answers with the questions.

1. 爸爸明天带我们去海滩玩，你知道吗？
2. 你有没有参加学校的足球队？
3. 我想参加跳舞比赛，要去哪里报名？
4. 你知道乒乓球比赛的日期吗？
5. 明天的比赛，我们的足球队会对哪队？

(　　) 是九月十四日上午十点。

(　　) 你可以跟陈老师说。

(　　) 知道，妈妈昨天跟我说了。

(　　) 中山学校。

(　　) 有，我们每星期四下午三点半练球。

拆拆看 What's in these characters?

Chinese characters are often made up of more than one word or radical.

For example: 时 is made up of 日 寸

Can you work out how the following characters are made up?

间 is made up of ....

报 is made up of ....

名 is made up of ....

加 is made up of ....

Now practise writing these characters.

报	报	报	报	报	报	报	报	报	报
名	名	名	名	名	名	名	名	名	名
参	参	参	参	参	参	参	参	参	参
加	加	加	加	加	加	加	加	加	加
队	队	队	队	队	队	队	队	队	队
对	对	对	对	对	对	对	对	对	对
舞	舞	舞	舞	舞	舞	舞	舞	舞	舞
赛	赛	赛	赛	赛	赛	赛	赛	赛	赛

第七课 C24/M69

周末不

Richard: Lata, 今天是周末, 不用上学。你做什么?

Lata: 今天早上十点, 我会先去图书馆借书, 然后跟Arun去溜冰场溜冰。溜完冰, 我们会去快餐店吃午饭。下午我们会去看电影。Richard, 你呢?

Sentence construction

To say that you will do something on a certain day or at a certain time, you use 会:

Time reference + Subject + 会+ activity

eg: 明天 + 我 + 会 + 去公园玩

⇨ 明天我会去公园玩。

eg: 今天下午 + 我 + 会 + 跟妈妈去买东西

⇨ 今天下午我会跟妈妈去买东西。

To say that you will do something after you have finished doing another thing, you put 完 after the verb, say 溜冰 where 溜 is the main verb:

eg: (溜冰) 溜完冰我们会去图书馆。

eg: (吃饭) 吃完饭我会看电视。

eg: (做功课) 做完功课我会踢足球。

一起来认字

C25/M70

周末 weekend	会 will	然后 afterwards
不用 no need to	先 first	先…然后 first… then…

Remember these phrases? 图书馆 超级市场 买东西 运动鞋
蛋糕 跟 带 弹琴 画画 看电影 教

用上学

Richard: 今天祖母来我家，她会教我们做蛋糕。我们会先去超级市场买东西，然后去鞋店买鞋。我的运动鞋太小了！买完鞋，我们回家做蛋糕。

To say that you will do something first, and then do another thing afterwards, you use 先…然后

Subject + 先 + activity + 然后 + activity

eg: 爸爸 + 先 + 去公园散步 + 然后 + 去看祖母

⇨ 爸爸先去公园散步，然后去看祖母。

To ask someone to lend something to you, you say:

我可以借你的书吗？

我可以借你的铅笔吗？

借 to borrow
溜冰 ice-skating
溜冰场 ice-skating rink
快餐店 fast food shop
完 finished
回家 return home
太 too

Question phrases to practise				
	谁	谁会来我家？	哪里	爸爸去哪里散步？
	什么	祖父来我家做什么？	几	今天是几月几日？

A. 画线连起来 Listen to the recording and draw lines to show who is borrowing what from whom. The first one is done for you.

Jamal	Richard
李大山	张马田
陈小玲	李月冬
Jasmine	Anna
Peter	Lata

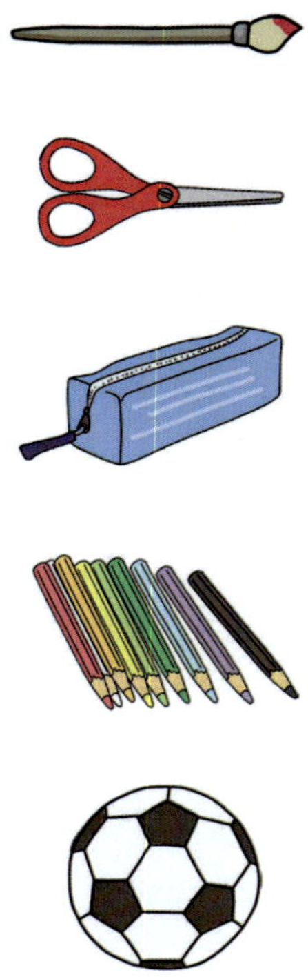

B. 画线连起来 Listen to the recording. Draw lines to link the person to the correct answer.

李月冬	做中文功课
张马田	游泳
陈小玲	睡觉
李大山	学弹琴

李老师：这个周末你们会做什么？

Richard：早上我会跟朋友踢足球，然后回家吃午饭。下午我会跟Chrissy去看电影。

张马田

李大山

Anna

这个周末，你会做什么？

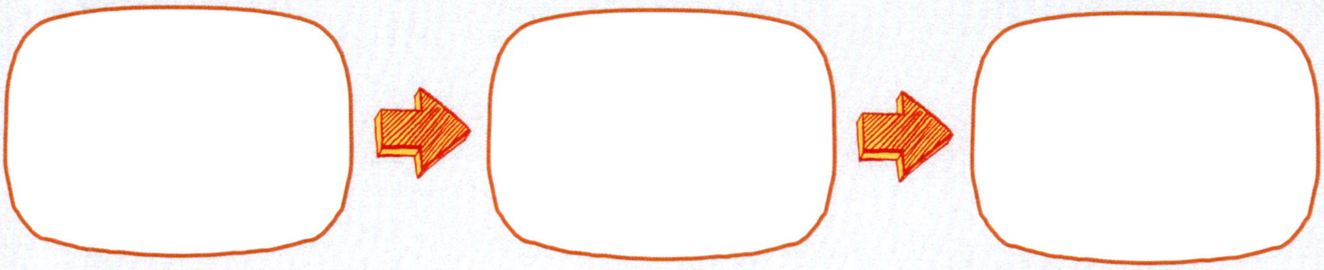

A. 找出正确答案

Match the Chinese with the English below.

(　) 溜冰场	(　) 图书馆
(　) 快餐店	(　) 玩具店
(　) 运动场	(　) 网球场

1. tennis court
2. library
3. sports ground
4. toy shop
5. fast food place
6. ice-skating rink

B. 填上正确答案

Find the correct answer to fill in the blanks.

今天是 ______ ______，不用上学。今天也是张美丽的生日，我们下午会去她的 ______ ______ ______。

早上我会先做 ______ ______，然后去 ______ ______ 买 ______ ______。下午我和月冬一起去美丽家。

生日会	周末	商店	功课	礼物

拆拆看 What's in these characters?

Chinese characters are often made up of more than one word or radical.

For example: 周 is made up of 用 口

Can you work out how the following characters are made up?

末 is made up of ……………………　　冰 is made up of ……………………

回 is made up of ……………………

Now practise writing these characters.

周	周	周	周	周	然	然	然	然	然
末	末	末	末	末	后	后	后	后	后
会	会	会	会	会	回	回	回	回	回
先	先	先	先	先	太	太	太	太	太
借	借	借	借	借	完	完	完	完	完

周末不

第八课 C28/M73

Anna 的爸爸周末不用上班。
他有空在家洗车和剪草。

李大山的爸爸
周末在家玩电
脑游戏。

Sentence construction

To ask a friend if s/he is free on a certain day or at a certain time, you say: subject + time + 有空吗?
eg. 你周末有空吗?
eg. 你今天下午有空吗?
eg. 你星期一有空吗?

To ask a friend what s/he would do when free at a certain time, you say:
周末有空，你会做什么?

一起来认字

C29/M74

有空 free

洗 wash

剪草 mow the lawn

电脑游戏 computer game

Remember these phrases? 图书馆 市场 超级市场

用上班

张马田的爸爸妈妈周末不用上班。他们会收拾房间和听音乐。星期日晚上张马田一家人常常到饭馆吃饭。

李大山的妈妈每个周末都去超级市场买菜。

To answer, you can say:
我会去看朋友。
eg. 今天下午有空，你会做什么？我会去公园放风筝。
eg. 明天有空，你会做什么？我会跟我妈妈去买东西。

买菜 shop for food　　房间 room　　饭馆 restaurant
收拾 tidy up　　音乐 music

Question phrases to practise	哪里	星期六有空，你会去哪里玩？	吗	你今天有空吗？
	什么	周末有空，你爸爸会做什么？		

A. 填上正确答案

Listen to the recording and write the correct number in the brackets in the order you hear it.

A (   )

B (   )

C (   )

D (   )

E (   )

F (   )

G (   )

H (   )

B. 填上正确答案 Listen to the recording and link the person to the correct activity.

李大山's dad (   )

陈小玲's mum (   )

Anna's mum (   )

Richard's dad (   )

Jasmine's family (   )

Anna's dad (   )

张马田's mum (   )

Lata's dad (   )

A

B

C

D

E

F

G

H

他们周末会做什么？What would they do on the weekend?

Anna 的妈妈会收拾房间。You can also say: Anna 的妈妈周末不用上班，她会收拾 Anna 和 Peter 的房间。

1

2

3

4

5

6

小调查 — 问问你的同学们他们的家人周末会做什么。

Now ask your friends what their parents would do in the weekends and then record your results in the table provided.

	爸爸	妈妈
收拾房间		
剪草		
洗车		
去买菜		
听音乐		
玩电脑游戏		

A. 找出正确答案

Match the pictures with the Chinese phrases given below:

1

2

3

4

5

6

7

8

(　　) 洗车　　(　　) 玩电脑游戏　　(　　) 剪草

(　　) 听音乐　　(　　) 买菜　　(　　) 溜冰

(　　) 收拾房间　　(　　) 吃晚饭

B. 填上正确答案 Fill in the blanks with the correct answers.

今天星期日，爸爸妈妈不用(　　　)。早上我和弟弟(　　　)帮他们(　　　)房间，(　　　)大家一起去超级市场(　　　)。买(　　　)菜，我们去(　　　)吃汉堡包。下午我(　　　)爸爸(　　　)，妈妈在花园(　　　)，弟弟跟小狗玩。晚上我们一家人去中国(　　　)吃饭。

收拾	上班	饭馆	帮	洗车	快餐店
剪草	然后	完	买菜	先	

拆拆看 What's in these characters?

Chinese characters are often made up of more than one word or radical.

For example: 空 is made up of 穴 and 工.

Can you work out how the following characters are made up?

洗 is made up of ……………………

游 is made up of ……………………

戏 is made up of ……………………

买 is made up of ……………………

菜 is made up of ……………………

听 is made up of ……………………

音 is made up of ……………………

乐 is made up of ……………………

Now practise writing these characters.

空	空	空	空	空	菜	菜	菜	菜	菜
洗	洗	洗	洗	洗	听	听	听	听	听
游	游	游	游	游	音	音	音	音	音
戏	戏	戏	戏	戏	乐	乐	乐	乐	乐
买	买	买	买	买	房	房	房	房	房

第九课 C31/M76

去餐厅

今天是祖父的生日。妈妈和妹妹做了一个草莓生日蛋糕送给他。

爸爸请他到餐厅吃饭。祖父喜欢吃烤牛肉和喝鸡汤。祖母也喜欢喝鸡汤。

Sentence construction

If someone has bought something to give you as a present, you say:
subject + 买了 + object + 送给 + someone
eg: 张马田买了一本书送给我。
eg: 祖母买了一个足球送给弟弟。

If someone has made something to give you as a present, you say:
subject + 做了 + object + 送给 + someone
eg: 张马田做了一个蛋糕送给他妈妈。
eg: 祖母做了一个风筝送给弟弟。

一起来认字

C32/M77

送给 to give as a gift
餐厅 restaurant
请 to treat
烤肉 roast meat

Remember these phrases? 生日 吃饭 喝 牛 羊 草莓 蛋糕

吃饭

爸爸和妈妈喜欢吃烤羊肉。妹妹喜欢吃炸鸡。
吃完饭后，我们一家人还去了电影院看电影。
大家都很高兴。

If someone has invited you to a restaurant as a treat, you say:
subject + 请 + someone + 去餐厅吃饭
eg: Anna的爸爸妈妈请我去餐厅吃饭。
eg: 李大山的妈妈请我和陈小玲去快餐店吃汉堡包。
eg: 今天Jasmine 请 Lata 吃蛋糕。

鸡 chicken	炸 deep fried	高兴 happy
汤 soup	还 also	

Question phrases to practise				
	谁	今天是谁的生日？	几	你们几个人去快餐店吃炸鸡？
	哪里	你们去哪里吃饭？	什么	弟弟送了什么给妹妹？

A. 填上正确答案

Listen to the recording and write the correct number in the brackets in the order you hear it.

(   )

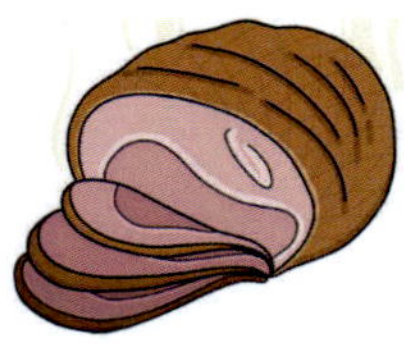

(   )

(   )

(   )

(   )

(   )

(   )

(   )

B. 用英文回答问题

Listen to the recording and answer the questions in English.

1. Whose birthday was yesterday? ....
2. Where did Lata and her family go for dinner? ....
3. What presents did Lata and her family give? ....
4. Where did Lata and her family go after dinner? ....
5. What did they do there? ....

A. 图画里的人吃什么？

What are the people in the picture eating?

1

2

B. 他们送什么礼物？ What are they giving as a present?

陈小玲的妈妈买了一件毛衣送给她。

1

2

3

4

Have you bought any present recently to give to your family or friend?

A. 找出正确答案

Match the pictures with the Chinese phrases given below:

1 

2 

3 

4 

5 

6 

7 

8 

蛋糕 (　　)	炸鸡 (　　)	米饭 (　　)	叉烧包 (　　)
面条 (　　)	春卷 (　　)	鸡汤 (　　)	烤牛肉 (　　)

B. 填上适当的词语 Fill in the blanks with the phrases given below.

1. 妈妈做了一个 .... 。
2. 祖父喜欢吃 .... 和喝 .... 。
3. 妹妹喜欢喝 .... 。
4. 爸爸在餐厅吃了 .... 和 .... 。
5. 吃完 .... 后，我们去看 .... 。
6. 弟弟最喜欢去 .... 吃 .... 。

快餐店	牛奶	蛋糕	炸鸡	面条
晚饭	烤牛肉	烤羊肉	电影	鸡汤

基本字形 Basic shapes

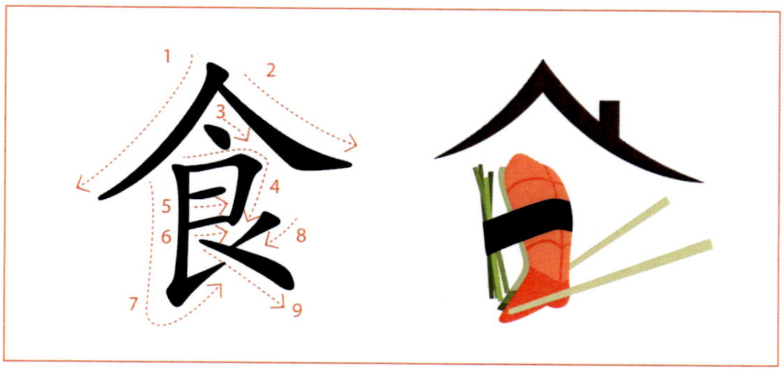

食 means to eat. When it is used as a radical, it looks like this: 饣. Can you see 饣 in 饭, 馆, 餐, 饮, 饱, 饿 ? Use a red pen to go over the 饣 in each character.

饭 馆 餐 饮 饱 饿

Now practise writing these characters.

送	送	送	送	送	请	请	请	请	请
给	给	给	给	给	鸡	鸡	鸡	鸡	鸡
饭	饭	饭	饭	饭	汤	汤	汤	汤	汤
餐	餐	餐	餐	餐	还	还	还	还	还
馆	馆	馆	馆	馆	肉	肉	肉	肉	肉

第十课　C35/M80

放暑假

李大山:
我和妹妹在暑假会去法国参加夏令营，我们会去四个星期。

张马田:
放暑假，我和姐姐会跟爸爸妈妈去香港旅游。在香港，我们会和祖父母见面。

Sentence construction

To say 放假 means to have a holiday.
To indicate what kind of holiday, you say 放xxx假.
eg: 放暑假，放圣诞假，
放中国新年假，放中秋节假

To tell someone that you go to some place for holiday (to sightsee), you say:
Subject + 去 + place + 度假
eg: 爸爸去中国度假
eg: 我们一家人去美国度假

一起来认字

C36/M81

暑假 summer holiday
夏令营 summer camp
参加 join
时候 time
度假 go on holiday
飞机 plane

Remember these phrases?　星期　爬山　最　高　坐　船　火车　汽车

陈小玲:
放假的时候，爸爸妈妈会带我去爬山，爬英国最高的山！

Jasmine:
我和哥哥会坐飞机去美国的迪士尼乐园度假。

You can use …的时候 to indicate when.
eg: When I am on holiday… 我放假的时候…
eg: When I am having my dinner… 我吃晚饭的时候…
eg: When I am watching TV… 我看电视的时候…

You can add '什么' before 时候 and it becomes 'when' – a question word!

旅游 tour round
见面 meet up
的时候 when
法国 France
香港 Hong Kong
迪士尼乐园 Disneyland
美国 America
英国 England

Question phrases to practise				
	哪里	暑假你去哪里？	什么时候	你什么时候去度假？
	怎么	你怎么去美国？	谁	你和谁一起去度假？

A. 填上正确答案

Write the correct numbers in the brackets as you hear them read out.

( ) ( ) ( ) ( )

B. 他们去哪里了？画线连起来？

Where did they go? Draw lines to link the person to the place.

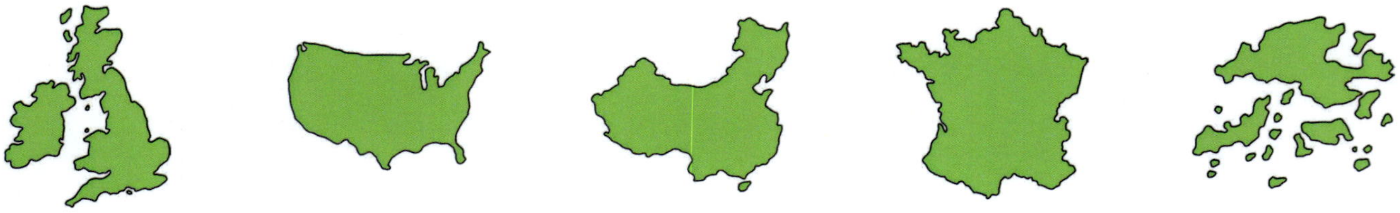

李大山 张马田 陈小玲 Jasmine Arun

C. 用英文回答问题

Listen to the recording and answer the questions in English.

1. Where did Jasmine go on holiday? ....
2. How did Jasmine get there? ....
3. Who went with Jasmine? ....
4. How long did they stay there? ....

Describe each picture below. Say who they are, where they are and what they do. You can say, for example:

王小明坐飞机去中国度假。

1

2

3

4

5

6

第十课

A. 这是什么国家？ Which countries are they?

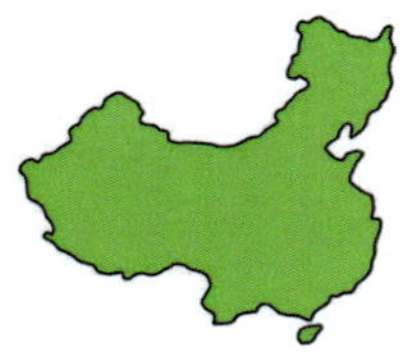

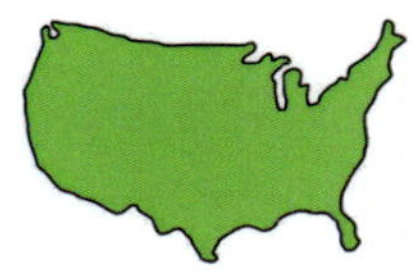

B. 放暑假你可以做什么？ Can you think of all the activities that you can do during the summer holidays.

	Activities 活动
第一个星期	
第二个星期	

1. 游泳
2. 去动物园
3. 参加夏令营
4. 帮妈妈剪草
5. 去爬山
6. 画画
7. 看书
8. 去旅行
9. 去看朋友
10. 打网球
11. 踢足球
12. 做运动
13. 做功课
14. 去公园
15. 学跳舞
16. 帮爸爸洗车

基本字形 Basic shapes

Remember 日 ? Here are a few characters containing this component:

时 暑 香 星

Now practise writing these characters.

时	时	时	时	时	时	时	时	时	时
暑	暑	暑	暑	暑	暑	暑	暑	暑	暑
假	假	假	假	假	假	假	假	假	假
香	香	香	香	香	香	香	香	香	香
港	港	港	港	港	港	港	港	港	港
星	星	星	星	星	星	星	星	星	星
期	期	期	期	期	期	期	期	期	期
飞	飞	飞	飞	飞	飞	飞	飞	飞	飞
机	机	机	机	机	机	机	机	机	机
候	候	候	候	候	候	候	候	候	候

写毛

文化（一） C39/M84

书法

Lata: 小玲, 你在做什么?

陈小玲: 我在写毛笔字。

Lata: 很好看! 写毛笔字难吗?

陈小玲: 不太难。我参加了一个书法班,
每星期六上一个小时课。

Sentence construction

To tell someone what you are doing right now, you use 在:

Subject + 在 + activity

eg: 我在写字　　eg: 妈妈在做饭

eg: 李月冬在画画　　eg: 张马田在弹琴

一起来认字

C40/M85

写 to write　　毛笔 brush pen

书法 calligraphy　　墨 black ink

Remember these phrases? 画画 唱歌 跳舞 网球

笔字

写毛笔字用
的文房四宝

Lata: 这是什么笔?
陈小玲: 这是毛笔，这是墨。
Lata: 我也可以写吗?
陈小玲: 好啊! 你跟着我写吧。

Using 小时 to indicate the length of time:
eg: 写一个小时毛笔字
eg: 弹半个小时琴
eg: 打一个小时羽毛球

Using 跟着 to ask someone to follow what you do:
eg: 跟着我唱歌
eg: 跟着老师写毛笔字
eg: 跟着爸爸画熊猫

纸 paper
难 difficult
班 class
小时 hour
跟着 follow

Question phrases to practise		
	什么时候	你什么时候上书法班?
	哪里	你在哪里上课?
	谁	谁教你跳舞?
	几	你每星期上几天课?
	怎么	你怎么写毛笔字?

文化（一） C41/M86

A. 填上正确答案

Write the correct numbers in the brackets as you hear them read out.

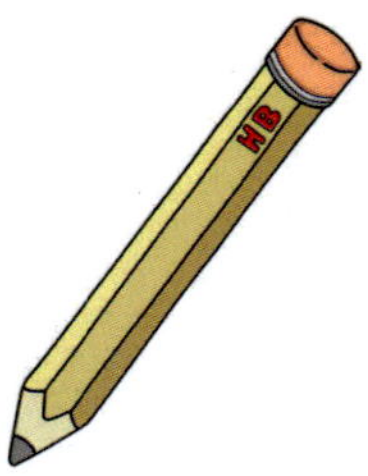
(　　)

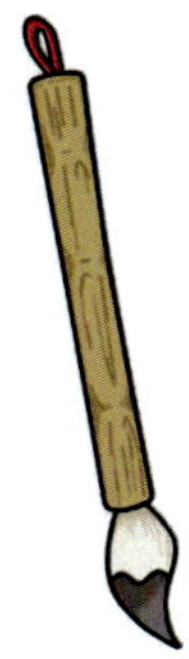
(　　)

(　　)

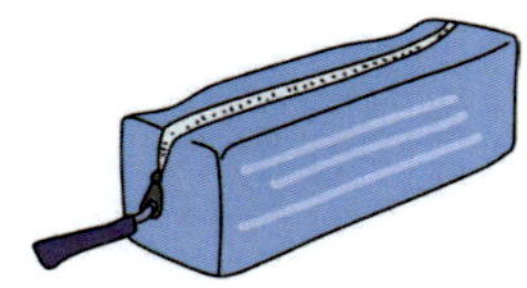
(　　)

B. 他们在做什么？ 把答案写在空格内

What are they doing? Write the answers in the boxes provided.

Jasmine

张马田

美丽

月冬

Richard

陈小玲

写毛笔字的四个要点 The four important points to follow when practising Chinese calligraphy.

STEP 1

To write Chinese calligraphy, you use a brush pen, ink and paper.
写毛笔字要用毛笔、墨和纸。

STEP 2

You should sit up straight when writing.
要坐好。

STEP 3

This is the correct way to hold a brush pen.
要这样拿笔。

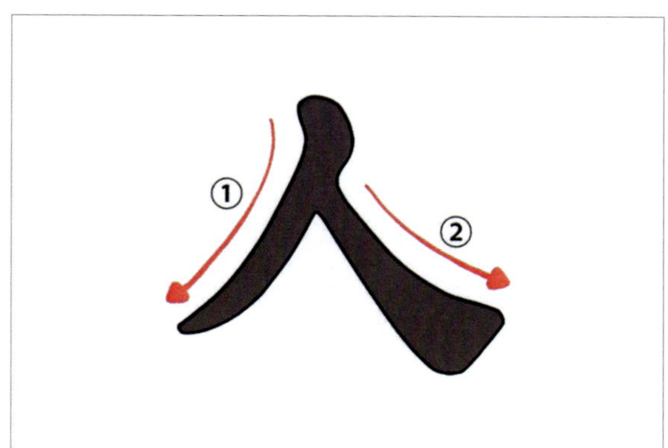

STEP 4

You must follow the stroke order when writing a character.
这样一笔一笔写:
第一笔, 第二笔...

Now you have a go at writing calligraphy. Afterwards try to follow the pictures above and explain to a friend how to do it in Chinese. (Practise with a partner. Pick a character which you want to show him/her the stroke order step by step.)

文化（一）

A. 找出正确答案

Match the Chinese with the correct picture below.

(　　)

(　　)

(　　)

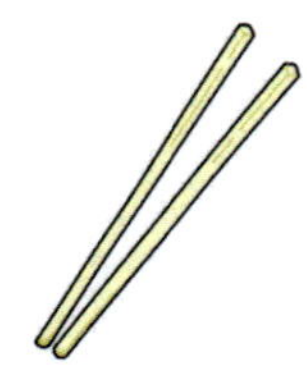
(　　)

(　　)

(　　)

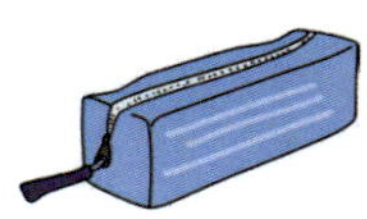
(　　)

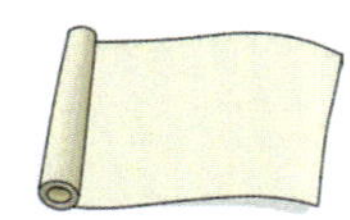
(　　)

1. 笔盒
2. 画画
3. 毛笔
4. 墨
5. 写字
6. 纸
7. 铅笔
8. 筷子

B. 参加哪个班?

Which class should they join? Write the name of the child next to the class.

a. 李大山 would like to learn to play table-tennis.
b. Chrissy would like to become a better swimmer.
c. 陈小玲 would like to learn to paint.
d. Anna likes dancing and would like to learn Chinese dance.
e. Arun is interested in Chinese calligraphy.
f. Jamal has never played badminton before and would like to learn to play.

学生	Activities 活动
	书法班
	游泳班
	羽毛球班
	画画班
	中国舞班
	乒乓球班

一起来写字

Remember these characters: 堆, 然, 戏, 级, 热, 对, 给, 鸡？ What does each one of these have in common with any of the characters below?

书 画 写 班

点 难 纸

Now practise writing these characters.

书	书	书	书	书	书	书	书	书	书
画	画	画	画	画	画	画	画	画	画
写	写	写	写	写	写	写	写	写	写
班	班	班	班	班	班	班	班	班	班
点	点	点	点	点	点	点	点	点	点
难	难	难	难	难	难	难	难	难	难
纸	纸	纸	纸	纸	纸	纸	纸	纸	纸

画中

Jasmine: 马田，你每星期日都来这里上国画班吗？
张马田: 是啊！我在这里学中文，也学画中国画。
那是张老师，她教我画画。
Jasmine: 你现在画什么？

Sentence construction

To say something resembles another thing, you use 像: A + 像 + B

eg: 妹妹像妈妈，弟弟像爸爸。
eg: 你画的猫像狗。
eg: 姐姐很像陈老师。

To say something about how you do in an activity, you use 得:

eg: 哥哥打网球打得很好。
eg: 姐姐唱歌唱得很好。
eg: 李大山溜冰溜得不好。

一起来认字

C43/M88

中国画/国画 Chinese painting
中文 Chinese
真 really
容易 easy

Remember these phrases? 画画 难 唱歌 跳舞 网球 溜冰

国画

张马田: 张老师今天教我们画鱼。我们用毛笔画。
你看，这像鱼吗？

Jasmine: 画得很好，真像一条鱼！中国画难学吗？

张马田: 不难！画画比写字容易！

To compare one activity with another using 比:

eg: 画画比写字容易。

eg: 写字比画画难。

eg: 跳舞比唱歌好玩。

A new question word to learn: 怎么样？

If you want to ask someone how you are doing in an activity, you say: 我画得怎么样？

To answer, you may say: 你画得很好

现在 now

像 look like/resemble

得

Question phrases to practise

哪里	你在哪里学中文？	什么时候	你什么时候上画画班？
谁	谁教你画中国画？	怎么样	你打羽毛球打得怎么样？

A. 填上正确答案

Write the correct numbers in the brackets as you hear them read out.

(   )

(   )

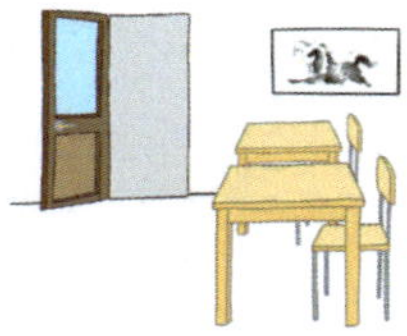
(   )

(   )

(   )

(   )

B. 找相反词

Listen to the recording and find the opposite of each phrase read out.

1. 大
2. 男
3. 高
4. 胖
5. 容易
6. 短

C. 回答问题 Listen to the recording and answer the questions.

1. Who goes ice-skating? ....
2. Who goes swimming? ....
3. Why does Martin not want to go ice-skating? ....
4. What does Chrissy like, swimming or skating? ....

A. 他们在做什么？

What are they doing?

1. 

2. 

3. 

4. 

5. 

B. 你最喜欢做什么活动？ What activity do you like best?

Chrissy: 美丽，你最喜欢做什么？

张美丽：我最喜欢打网球。我参加了一个网球班，每星期去运动场上课。我也跟爸爸一起打网球，每个周末，我们都去网球场打。

Now choose an activity you like best and tell your partner about it.

A. 找出正确答案

Match the English with the correct Chinese phrases below.

现在(　)　难(　)　高(　)　容易(　)　像(　)　真(　)

1. tall　2. difficult　3. look like　4. really　5. now　6. easy

B. 填上正确答案 Fill in the blanks with one of the phrases given.

1. ________七点半了，你要起床上学了。
2. 妈妈每天都带小狗去公园散步一个________。
3. 这个中文字很________，你可以帮我吗？
4. 李苹：这个女孩子很________王老师！

   Janet：是啊！王老师是她的妈妈。
5. 你爸爸做的蛋糕________好吃！
6. Chrissy会画________，她画的花和鸟都很好看。
7. Amir 会写________，他用________和________写。
8. 溜冰比打网球________，我喜欢溜冰。
9. 上课的时候，学生们________老师学中文。

现在	难	真	毛笔字	跟着	墨
容易	像	国画	小时	毛笔	

一起来写字

Remember 场 and 踢? Now look at 易 and see if you can find anything in common in these three characters.

場 踢 易

Now practise writing these characters.

易	易	易	易	易	易	易	易	易	易
场	场	场	场	场	场	场	场	场	场
现	现	现	现	现	现	现	现	现	现
像	像	像	像	像	像	像	像	像	像
得	得	得	得	得	得	得	得	得	得
真	真	真	真	真	真	真	真	真	真
容	容	容	容	容	容	容	容	容	容

故事（第一课） 可以不可以

CS/M50

今天上中文课，老师和学生温习生词。他把四个未完成的句子写在左边，然后叫学生用学过的词语来完成句子。

张马田完成第一句：我们可以在教室打乒乓球。

Lata 完成第二句：我们可以在运动场看书。

Jasmine 完成第三句：我们可以在图书馆睡觉。

Richard 成第四句：我们可以在礼堂吃东西。

老师觉得很奇怪，原来学生会用教室、运动场和图书馆做其他活动！

故事（第九课） 石头汤的故事

C34/M79

从前有一个过路人来到一个老婆婆家里借地方住和找食物。过路人说：「我有一块神奇的石头,可以做出美味的汤!」

过路人一边煮一边说：「真香! 我最喜欢喝石头汤, 不过, 如果加些胡萝卜, 味道就会更鲜美!」

老婆婆被他说得也有一点儿肚饿了, 于是把胡萝卜拿出来, 给过路人放入锅里。过路人尝一口汤, 他说：「味道真好!我以前喝过加了肉的石头胡萝卜汤, 那个味道好得难以形容!」

老婆婆被他说得心动了, 她从橱柜里拿出一块咸牛肉来给过路人放入锅里。

过路人说：「哗! 真好味! 这个汤比我以前喝过的更好味道! 如果再加一些洋葱就更加好了!」

就这样, 老婆婆从橱柜拿出洋葱、芹菜等等给过路人放入锅里。最后, 汤做好了, 他们坐在一起喝汤。

老婆婆说：「真好味! 我从未喝过这样好味道的汤! 你愿意把你的石头卖给我吗?」

过路人说：「对不起,这块石头只有跟着我的时候, 才会做出美味的汤。以后我再路过这里的话, 我一定带着石头来你家再做汤给你喝!」

故事（第十课） 小狗去旅行

C38/M83

张马田一家人计划去外国度假，他们不可以带小狗美美一起去。马田问朋友们可以不可以帮忙照顾美美。

李大山说他们一家人也去度假，他们会去中国度假。

Richard 说他们一家人也去度假，他们会去法国度假。

Lata 说他们一家人也去度假，他们会去美国度假。

张马田的爸爸妈妈没有办法，只好改变计划。

他们一家人不去外国度假了，他们会去英国海滩度假，小狗美美也可以一起去了。

故事（画国画） 画龙点睛

C45/M90

一位画家在墙上画了三条龙，大家都称赞他画得很生动。

怎么这三条龙没有画上眼睛呢？

画家说：「画上眼睛，龙就会飞上天了。」

大家都不相信，一定要他给龙画上眼睛。画家只好拿起画笔，给一条龙点上眼睛。

这时，天空立刻打雷闪电，点上眼睛的一条龙冲出墙壁，飞到天上去了。

大家定下神来看看，墙壁上只剩下两条没有点上眼睛的龙。

一起来唱歌 （第二课） 今天下雨

C9/M54

1. 今天晴天去海滩，
去海滩，做什么？
今天晴天去海滩，
去海滩，晒太阳。

2. 今天下雪去公园，
去公园，做什么？
今天下雪去公园，
去公园，堆雪人。

3. 今天有风上高山，
上高山，做什么？
今天有风上高山，
上高山，放风筝。

4. 今天下雨留在家，
留在家，做什么？
今天下雨留在家，
留在家，睡大觉！

金头发 蓝眼睛

C16/M61

1. 金头发，蓝眼睛，
穿高鞋，戴围巾，
这是我的绿老师。

2. 黑头发，棕眼睛，
穿长裤，戴帽子，
这是我的黄老师。

3. 红头发，绿眼睛，
穿短裙，戴眼镜，
这是我的白老师。

4. 金黑红，蓝棕绿，
穿红穿绿穿黄白，
都是我们的老师。

我有个好姐姐

C20/M65

1. 我有个好姐姐，
不胖不瘦很美丽。
我有个好姐姐，
我爱我的好姐姐。

2. 我有个好哥哥，
又高又大很精神。
我有个好哥哥，
我爱我的好哥哥。

3. 我有个好弟弟，
会跑会跳真淘气。
我有个好弟弟，
我爱我的好弟弟。

4. 我有个好妹妹，
会说会唱真可爱。
我有个好妹妹，
我爱我的好妹妹。

一起来唱歌（第七课）周末放假

C27/M72

1. 周末放假真高兴，
去打网球和溜冰，
吃完快餐看电影，
天气好时去露营。

2. 周末放假真高兴，
去放风筝和游泳，
吃完点心看电影，
天气好时去露营。

Vocabulary

Vocabulary	English meaning	Putonghua pinyin	Cantonese jyutping
CHAPTER 1			
多	many	duō	do1
图书馆	library	tú shū guǎn	tou4 syu1 gun2
教室 / 课室	classroom	jiào shì / kè shì	gaau3 sat1 / fo3 sat1
礼堂	assembly hall	lǐ táng	lai5 tong4
食堂 / 饭堂	canteen	shí táng / fàn táng	sik6 tong4 / faan6 tong4
室	room	shì	sat1
教	teach	jiào	gaau3
百	hundred	bǎi	baak3
可以	can	kě yǐ	ho2 ji5
上课	attend lesson	shàng kè	soeng5 fo3
CHAPTER 2			
晴天	clear day	qíng tiān	cing4 tin1
下雨	rain	xià yǔ	haa6 jyu5
下雪	snow	xià xuě	haa6 syut3
有风	windy	yǒu fēng	jau5 fung1
阴天	cloudy	yīn tiān	jam1 tin1
下毛毛雨	drizzle	xià máo máo yǔ	haa6 mou4 mou4 jyu5
爬山	to climb mountain	pá shān	paa4 saan1
堆	to pile up	duī	deoi1
雪人	snowman	xuě rén	syut3 jan4
CHAPTER 3			
季节	season	jì jié	gwai3 zit3
最	most	zuì	zeoi3
春天	Spring	chūn tiān	ceon1 tin1
秋天	Autumn	qiū tiān	cau1 tin1
天气	weather	tiān qì	tin1 hei3
暖	warm	nuǎn	nyun5
凉	cool	liáng	loeng4
叶	leaf	yè	jip6

Vocabulary	English meaning	Putonghua pinyin	Cantonese jyutping
满是	covered with/full of	mǎn shì	mun^{5} si^{6}
十分	extremely	shí fēn	sap^{6} fan^{1}
美丽	beautiful	měi lì	mei^{5} lai^{6}
CHAPTER 4			
高	tall	gāo	gou^{1}
矮	short	ǎi	ai^{2}
胖	fat	pàng	bun^{6}
瘦	slim	shòu	sau^{3}
个子	build	gè zi	go^{3} zi^{2}
男	male	nán	naam^{4}
棕色	brown	zōng sè	zung^{1} sik^{1}
漂亮	pretty	piào liàng	piu^{3} loeng^{6}
头发	hair	tóu fà	tau^{4} faat^{3}
眼镜	eye-glasses	yǎn jìng	ngaan^{5} geng^{2}
CHAPTER 5			
祖父	grandfather	zǔ fù	zou^{2} fu^{6}
祖母	grandmother	zǔ mǔ	zou^{2} mou^{5}
讲	to tell, say	jiǎng	gong^{2}
比	compare	bǐ	bei^{2}
慈祥	kind	cí xiáng	ci^{4} coeng^{4}
跟	with/and	gēn	gan^{1}
常常	often	cháng cháng	soeng^{4} soeng^{4}
孩子	child	hái zi	haai^{4} zi^{2}
爱	love	ài	oi^{3}
CHAPTER 6			
比赛	match/competition	bǐ sài	bei^{2} coi^{3}
队	team/group	duì	deoi^{6}
队员	team member	duì yuán	deoi^{6} jyun^{4}
对	against	duì	deoi^{3}

Vocabulary

Vocabulary	English meaning	Putonghua pinyin	Cantonese jyutping
知道	to know	zhī dào	zi1 dou6
对不起	sorry	duì bù qǐ	deoi3 bat1 hei2
报名	register	bào míng	bou3 meng2
参加	take part	cān jiā	caam1 gaa1
跳舞	to dance	tiào wǔ	tiu3 mou5
练习	to practise	liàn xí	lin6 zaap6
CHAPTER 7			
周末	weekend	zhōu mò	zau1 mut6
不用	no need to	bú yòng	bat1 jung6
会	will	huì	wui6
先	first	xiān	sin1
然后	afterwards	rán hòu	jin4 hau6
先…然后…	first…then…	xiān …rán hòu	sin1…jin4 hau6…
借	to borrow	jiè	ze3
溜冰	ice-skating	liū bīng	lau6 bing1
溜冰场	ice-skating rink	liū bīng chǎng	lau6 bing1 coeng4
完	finished	wán	jyun4
快餐店	fast food shop	kuài cān diàn	faai3 caan1 dim3
回家	to return home	huí jiā	wui4 gaa1
太	too	tài	taai3
CHAPTER 8			
有空	free	yǒu kòng	jau5 hung1
洗	to wish	xǐ	sai2
剪草	to mow the lawn	jiǎn cǎo	zin2 cou2
电脑游戏	computer game	diàn nǎo yóu xì	din6 nou5 jau4 hei3
买菜	to shop for food	mǎi cài	maai5 coi3
收拾	tidy up	shōu shí	sau1 sap6
房间	room	fáng jiān	fong4 gaan1
音乐	music	yīn yuè	jam1 ngok6
饭馆	restaurant	fàn guǎn	faan6 gun2

Vocabulary	English meaning	Putonghua pinyin	Cantonese jyutping
CHAPTER 9			
送给	to give as a gift	sòng gěi	$sung^3\ kap^1$
请	to treat	qǐng	$ceng^2$
餐厅	restaurant	cān tīng	$caan^1\ teng^1$
烤肉	roast meat	kǎo ròu	$haau^1\ juk^6$
鸡	chicken	jī	gai^1
汤	soup	tāng	$tong^1$
炸	deep fried	zhá	zaa^3
还	also	hái	$waan^4$
高兴	happy	gāo xìng	gou1 $hing^3$
CHAPTER 10			
暑假	summer holiday	shǔ jià	$syu^2\ gaa^3$
放暑假	holiday	fàng shǔ jià	$fong^3\ syu^2\ gaa^3$
参加	to join	cān jiā	$caam^1\ gaa^1$
夏令营	summer camp	xià líng yíng	haa6 $ling^6\ jing^4$
香港	Hong Kong	xiāng gǎng	$hoeng^1\ gong^2$
旅游	to tour around	lǚ yóu	$leoi^5\ jau^4$
见面	meet up	jiàn miàn	$gin^3\ min^6$
时候	time	shí hòu	$si^4\ hau^6$
…的时候	when…	de shí hòu	…dik $si^4\ hau^6$
飞机	aeroplane	fēi jī	$fei^1\ gei^1$
美国	America	měi guó	$mei^5\ gwok^3$
英国	Britain	yīng guó	$jing^1\ gwok^3$
法国	France	fǎ guó	$faat^3\ gwok^3$
迪士尼乐园	Disneyland	díshìní lè yuán	$dik^6\ si^6\ nei^4\ lok^6\ jyun^4$
度假	to go on holiday	dù jià	$dou^6\ gaa^3$

Vocabulary

Vocabulary	English meaning	Putonghua pinyin	Cantonese jyutping
CULTURE 1			
写	to write	xiě	se^2
书法	calligraphy	shū fǎ	syu^1 faat^3
毛笔	brush pen	máo bǐ	mou^4 bat^1
墨	black ink	mò	mak^6
纸	paper	zhǐ	zi^2
难	difficult	nán	naan^4
班	class	bān	baan^1
小时	hour	xiǎo shí	siu^2 si^4
跟着	to follow	gēn zhe	gan^1 zoek^6
CULTURE 2			
中国画/国画	Chinese painting	zhōng guóhuà/ guó huà	zung^1 gwok^3 waa^6/ gwok^3 waa^6
中文	Chinese	zhōng wén	zung^1 man^4
现在	now	xiàn zài	jin^6 zoi^6
像	look like/resemble	xiàng	zoeng^6
得		dé	dak^1
真	really	zhēn	zan^1
容易	easy	róng yì	jung^4 ji^6

目录 Contents

Chrissy's family

李大山家

Jamal's family